HEALTH & FITNESS

EXERCISE

Judy Sadgrove

RSVP

RAINTREE
STECK-VAUGHN
PUBLISHERS
A Steck-Vaughn Company

Austin, Texas

www.steck-vaughn.com

ADOLESCENCE
DIET AND NUTRITION
DRINKING, SMOKING, AND OTHER DRUGS
EXERCISE

Published by Raintree Steck-Vaughn Publishers, an imprint of Steck-Vaughn Company

Library of Congress Cataloging-in-Publication Data
Sadgrove, Judy.
Exercise / Judy Sadgrove.
    p.   cm.—(Health & fitness)
    Includes bibliographical references and index.
    Summary: Describes the importance of regular exercise in maintaining health and physical fitness and provides tips on choosing an activity.
    ISBN 0-7398-1347-1
    1. Exercise—Juvenile literature.
    2. Physical fitness—Juvenile literature.
    [1. Exercise. 2. Physical fitness.]
    I. Title. II. Series.
    QR301.S135   2000
    613.7'1—dc21   99-32659

Printed in Italy. Bound in the United States.
1 2 3 4 5 6 7 8 9 0 04 03 02 01 00

Picture acknowledgments:
Digital Stock *front cover band* bottom; Digital Vision *front cover band* middle, 6, 8, 16, 17, 36, 38 top, 40 top; Image bank 43 top (Marc Romanelli), Science Photo Library 18 top (BSIP Vem), 21 (Scott Camazine), 35 (Biophoto), 44 (Oscar Burriel/Latin Stock); Tony Stone Images *front cover* main image, 1 (Terry Vine), 5 (David Young Wolff), 7 (Lori Adamski Peek), 12 (Bruce Ayres), 13 (Amwell), 14 (Amwell), 15 (Dave Rosenberg), 19 (Ian O'Leary), 20 (Bill Robbins), 22 (James Darrell), 23 (Al Bello), 24 (Bob Torrez), 25 (Penny Tweedie), 26 (Amwell), 28 (Bill Truslow), 31 (Bruce Ayres), 37 (Robert Aschenbrenner), 38 bottom (Terry Vine), 40 bottom (John McDermott), 42 (Bob Torrez), 45 top (Bruce Ayres), 45 bottom (David Madison); John Walmsley Photography 4, 10, 27, 29, 30-31, 34; Wayand Picture Library 18 bottom. The artwork on the cover and page 9 is by Peter Bull. The artwork on page 11 is by Alex Pang. The artwork on pages 32-33 is by Michael Posen.

CONTENTS

WHY DO WE NEED EXERCISE?

In ancient times, our ancestors constantly roamed the landscape in search of food. But today we spend most of our lives sitting down—in cars and buses, at school, at home, and in front of TVs and computers. This inactive lifestyle causes major health problems, because the human body has evolved to stay on the move.

USE IT OR LOSE IT

An unused body deteriorates, just like a rusty old bike abandoned by the roadside. If we sit around all day long and don't use our bodies, we will soon lose our physical fitness. Being chronically unfit causes changes in the heart, lungs, blood, bones, and muscles that will eventually harm our health.

UNFIT EQUALS UNHEALTHY

People who are unfit are more likely to have heart attacks when they are older. They are also more likely to develop other serious diseases. Lack of exercise is also the most important reason why so many of us—children and adults—are overweight.

WHY BOTHER WITH EXERCISE?

You may feel fine just sitting around, but bodies are designed to move. And if you become more active, you will feel much better. Exercise makes you more fit, keeps you slimmer, gives you more energy, helps you look good, and cheers you up. And what's more, it's fun.

WHAT IS EXERCISE?

Some people excel at school sports, while others don't. Luckily, exercise doesn't just mean team games. It is any form of physical activity, from roller-blading to martial arts, yoga, table tennis, cycling, ice skating, dancing, or simply walking.

MOVE THAT BODY!

Because most of us sit down for so much of the time, the more we all move around, the more fit we will become. But there's more to exercise than that. You can learn to train your body so that it will look its best and give the best possible performance at whatever you enjoy doing most.

Right Basketball is fun, but it is also good for you. It can make you more agile, help build up your bones, and increase your leg strength.

Below Many of the things we enjoy doing—such as playing computer games or watching TV—involve sitting down, so we need to exercise to keep our bodies in shape.

WHAT IS FITNESS?

To be physically fit, we need to be fit in three areas. These are called aerobic fitness, muscular fitness, and flexibility. You may have heard them described as the three "S"s—stamina, strength, and suppleness.

Swimming is good aerobic exercise, but to really give the heart and lungs a good workout you need to swim lengths rather than just splashing around.

WHAT IS AEROBIC FITNESS?

If you find that you have to catch your breath halfway up a long flight of stairs, then you may need to improve your aerobic fitness. This is the ability to keep going (your stamina) at any rhythmic activity that uses large muscles and makes you breathless. You can improve your aerobic fitness by getting more aerobic exercise.

WHAT IS AEROBIC EXERCISE?

Activity that works the heart and lungs, such as brisk walking, jogging, and swimming, is known as aerobic exercise. The energy for this type of exercise comes mostly from your body fat. It is released when your body "burns" this fat in the presence of oxygen taken in by breathing. ("Aerobic" means in the presence of oxygen.)

BENEFITS OF AEROBIC EXERCISE

Aerobic exercise is good for your heart because when you jog or swim, your heart has to work harder than usual, pumping blood to work your muscles. This hard work makes it stronger and more fit. If you keep your heart fit, then you'll be less likely to develop heart disease when you are older. This is why it's so important to get regular aerobic exercise throughout your life.

AND THAT'S NOT ALL ...

Aerobic exercise also helps keep you slim. The oxygen you take in as you puff and pant allows the fat stored in your body to be burned to produce energy for your muscles. Getting enough aerobic exercise will keep you from becoming overweight and help you lose fat if you already weigh too much. You may have heard aerobic exercise being described as "fat-burning" exercise.

Right Working out in a step class. If you don't like exercising alone, step classes are an enjoyable way of improving your aerobic fitness. Step aerobics can also help keep you slim by burning up body fat.

HOW AEROBIC EXERCISE WORKS

When you jog for several minutes, your heart beats faster and you breathe more quickly and deeply to get more oxygen into your system. The oxygen is carried away from your lungs by your blood. The heart pumps this freshly oxygenated blood first to the heart itself and then to all the tissues of the body, including your working leg muscles. The blood travels through blood vessels called arteries, which divide into smaller and smaller tubes called arterioles and finally tiny capillaries.

OXYGEN EXCHANGE

At the capillary level, the cells of your muscles and all other body tissues pick up the oxygen they need to carry out many vital tasks, including producing energy to keep your body moving. In exchange for the oxygen, the cells dump a waste product, carbon dioxide, back into the blood.

Speed cycling is an intense form of aerobic exercise. In speed races, cyclists reach speeds of more than 30 mph (50 km/h).

EXAMPLES OF AEROBIC EXERCISE

★ Brisk walking
★ Jogging and distance running
★ Swimming
★ Aerobics and step classes
★ Cycling
★ Rowing
★ Dancing
★ Cardiomachines, such as the stepper, exercise bike, and rower
★ Team sports have some aerobic benefits

WASTE DISPOSAL

This deoxygenated blood returns to the heart through capillaries and other blood vessels called venules and veins. From the heart it goes back to the lungs, where the carbon dioxide is released. As you breathe out, you expel the carbon dioxide and as you breathe in, you take in oxygen, which replenishes your blood. Then the whole process begins again.

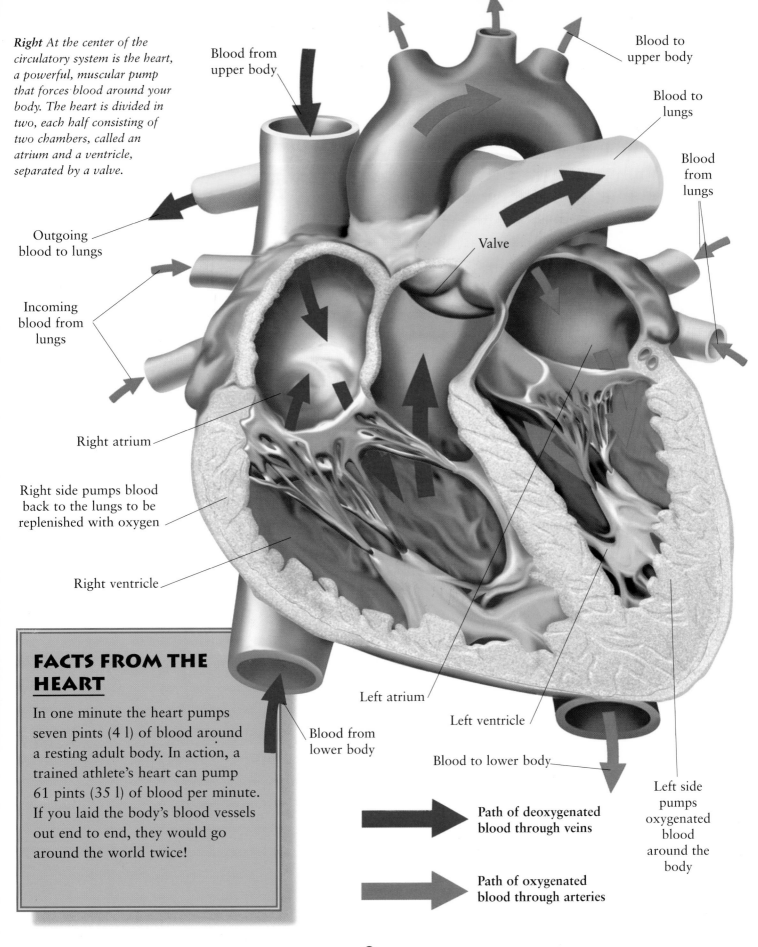

Right At the center of the circulatory system is the heart, a powerful, muscular pump that forces blood around your body. The heart is divided in two, each half consisting of two chambers, called an atrium and a ventricle, separated by a valve.

Blood from upper body

Blood to upper body

Blood to lungs

Blood from lungs

Outgoing blood to lungs

Valve

Incoming blood from lungs

Right atrium

Right side pumps blood back to the lungs to be replenished with oxygen

Right ventricle

Left atrium

Left ventricle

FACTS FROM THE HEART

In one minute the heart pumps seven pints (4 l) of blood around a resting adult body. In action, a trained athlete's heart can pump 61 pints (35 l) of blood per minute. If you laid the body's blood vessels out end to end, they would go around the world twice!

Blood from lower body

Blood to lower body

Left side pumps oxygenated blood around the body

Path of deoxygenated blood through veins

Path of oxygenated blood through arteries

EXAMPLES OF ANAEROBIC EXERCISE

★ Lifting free-weights (barbells and dumbbells)
★ Using resistance machines
★ Floor exercises, such as push-ups and abdominal curls
★ Toning and conditioning classes
★ Sprinting, jumping, and other power moves

MUSCULAR FITNESS

If you find it hard to lift a weight that your friends can lift with ease, you may lack muscular fitness, which consists of strength and muscular endurance. Strength is the ability of your muscles to lift weights or perform power moves, such as jumping. Muscular endurance is your muscles' ability to keep working, as in rowing, cycling, or skiing.

MUSCLES UNDER STRESS

You can improve muscular fitness by doing exercises that stress your muscles. Using resistance machines or lifting free-weights in the gym is good for this. Alternatively, you can work against the weight of your body by doing floor exercises, such as press-ups and abdominal curls.

Left "Pumping iron" in a gym improves anaerobic fitness, making muscles stronger and able to work longer.

Triceps relaxes and lengthens to allow forearm to be raised

Triceps and biceps muscles of upper arm form an opposing pair

ANAEROBIC EXERCISE

Exercise that makes your muscles more fit and stronger is called anaerobic (without oxygen) exercise. The main fuel used in anaerobic exercise is your body's store of carbohydrate (glycogen). Explosive work, such as power lifts or short sprints, uses a different energy source—creatine phosphate, a substance that your muscles store in small quantities.

Biceps relaxes and lengthens

Triceps contracts to straighten out the elbow

Biceps muscle contracts, pulling on forearm

Forearm flexes

HOW MUSCLES WORK

There are about 600 muscles in your body. They support your skeleton and enable you to move your joints. Muscles work in balanced pairs, like the biceps and triceps muscles in your arm. When you bend your arm up from the elbow, the biceps at the front of your upper arm shortens to do the work. When a muscle does this it is called a prime mover. At the same time, the triceps at the back of your arm lengthens. It is called the antagonist. When you straighten your arm, the roles are reversed: the triceps muscle shortens, becoming the prime mover, and the biceps muscle lengthens, so it becomes the antagonist.

Always train both muscles in every pair—the front and back of the legs, the abdomen, and the back muscles—otherwise imbalances occur that cause injuries.

Muscles can only pull on your bones, not push them, so they are arranged in opposing pairs. When one muscle contracts, the other relaxes and lengthens.

Forearm extends

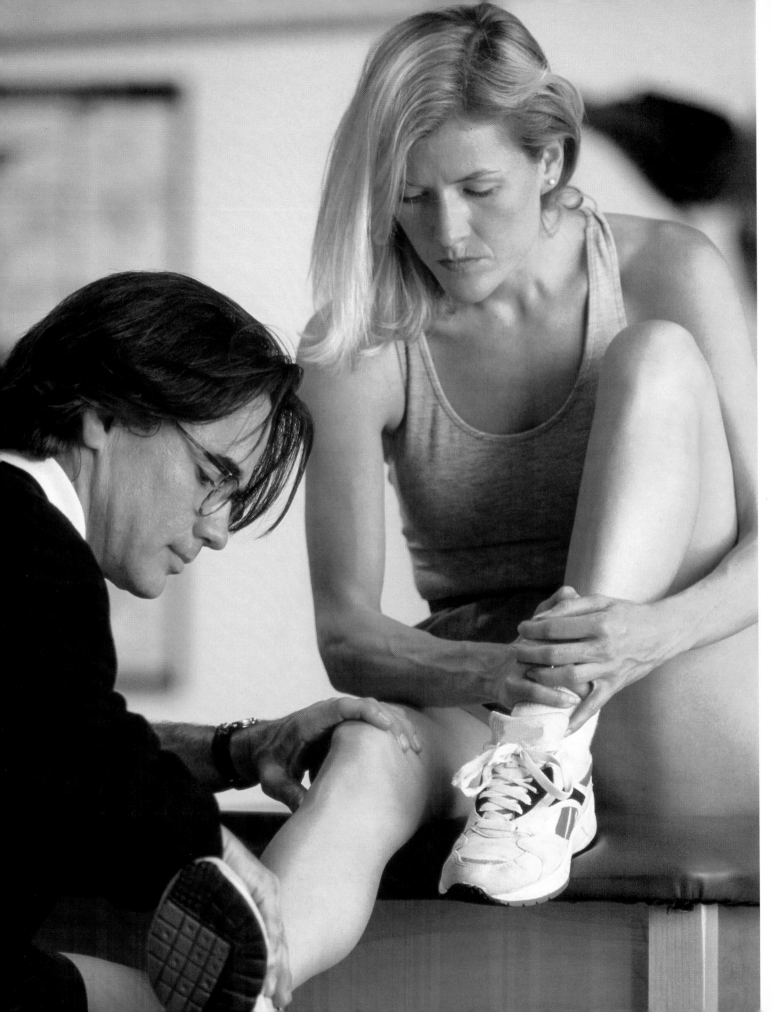

Right Championship power lifters can raise incredibly heavy loads, as much as five times their own body weight.

WARNING!

Never lift heavy weights. Young bones are soft because they are still growing. They can be bent or twisted if you overdevelop certain muscles, so you should not lift heavy weights until you are at least 18. Instead, do lots of reps (repetitions) with lighter weights.

BENEFITS OF ANAEROBIC EXERCISE

Improving your muscular fitness makes you stronger, so ordinary tasks become easier. Because muscle cells produce energy, having more muscle makes you feel more energetic. Greater muscular fitness also helps keep you slim. Having more muscle boosts your metabolic rate—the rate at which your body carries out its normal functions—so that you use more calories even when you're watching TV.

MORE MUSCLES, LESS INJURY

The better your muscular fitness, the greater protection you'll have against injury. The more muscle you have, the easier movement becomes, and the less likely you are to have an accident. Muscle also acts like a cushion, protecting bones and joints when you fall. Finally, improving muscular fitness helps build up bone. Muscles pull on bone, so when you work your muscles, you also strengthen your bones.

TRAINING TIPS

★ Always work both muscles in each pair.
★ Work all the body's major muscles, so that you don't create imbalance.
★ Train in a supervised gym, where the instructor will show you how to adjust the machines.
★ Check your posture in a mirror.
★ Keep joints aligned—knees in line with ankles and toes, and shoulders, hips, and wrists straight.
★ Always bend your legs (not your back) to lift free-weights.

Left A sports doctor examines an athlete's leg. Building more muscle makes accidents and injuries less likely.

DID YOU KNOW?

LACTIC ACID

In anaerobic exercise, your muscles soon get sore and tired so you have to stop. This is caused by a build-up of lactic acid, a substance produced in the muscles when carbohydrate is burned for fuel. After a minute or two, the lactic acid is dispersed by the blood system and you can continue exercising.

THE BENEFITS OF STRETCHING

Stretching before exercise prepares your muscles for work and reduces the risk of injury. Short, tight muscles are more likely to be injured than long, elastic ones. Stretching afterward helps your muscles recover by lengthening them after they have contracted during exercise. It also prevents soreness over the next couple of days. The best time to work on your flexibility is after exercise, because your muscles are already warmed up.

STRETCH WHENEVER YOU CAN

Get into the habit of stretching when you get up in the morning and when you stand up after a period of sitting. You can stretch while sitting at your desk, while watching TV, and even while lying in bed.

FLEXIBILITY

Can you touch your toes when you sit on the floor with your legs straight out in front of you? If not, you might want to improve your flexibility, which is the ability to move your joints through their full range of movement. Flexibility, or suppleness, is vital for the future. Some old people get so stiff that they can't bend down to cut their toenails. And while you're young, being flexible makes you more graceful—think of gymnasts, martial artists, and ballet dancers.

IMPROVING FLEXIBILITY

You can improve your flexibility by stretching. Stretching lengthens and relaxes your muscles so that they become more elastic, allowing your joints to pass through a wider range of movement. In general, women are more supple than men, and girls tend to be more supple than boys—but this may be simply because many girls work more on their flexibility, especially if they perform gymnastics or go to dance classes.

YOGA

Yoga consists of hundreds of different stretches, some simple, some very difficult. These stretches are called asanas, and they are often based on the movements of animals. Practicing yoga improves flexibility, strength, and posture and encourages serenity.

HOW EXERCISE CAN HELP YOU

If you get more exercise you will soon start feeling better than you do now. This is because exercise has a profound impact on the body, making it healthier in many different ways. Some of the physical benefits of regular exercise are listed here.

Skiing is a great activity for improving leg strength and reflexes, but high-speed downhill competition skiing like this is not for the timid!

1. GENERAL FITNESS

You can only become as fit as your genes will allow you to be. But if you discover that your body fitness level is 75 percent or less, you will definitely notice an improvement. As your fitness increases, you will find that you can keep going at all physical activities for longer and that you will feel less tired generally.

2. SPECIFIC FITNESS

Whatever exercise you take up, you will become better at it provided that you do it regularly. If you take up running, for example, you will soon become a good runner. This will not make you into a good swimmer—unless, of course, you also swim regularly. You only become good at the activities you do.

3. MOTOR FITNESS

Your motor fitness includes skills such as speed, power, agility, coordination, balance, and reaction times. If your chosen activity includes any of these skills, they will naturally improve. You can also work on them with specific exercises, such as sprints to build up speed, jumps to build up leg power, and weaving back and forth as you run to build up agility.

4. IMMUNE SYSTEM

Getting enough exercise strengthens your immune system, which fights off infection.

5. HEART

When you take regular aerobic exercise, your heart actually grows in size. This improves the oxygen supply to the heart's muscles and makes the heart more efficient.

The high jump suits people who are tall, lean, and flexible. Top high jumpers can clear bars around 8 ft. (2.5 m) high.

It can slow down and work less hard, which means you're less likely to have a heart attack when you're older. If you are aerobically fit, you will have a lower heart rate than someone who is unfit.

6. BLOOD SYSTEM

Doing regular aerobic exercise helps your blood flow smoothly around your body by bringing down your cholesterol level. Cholesterol is a type of fat found in the blood. When you don't get enough exercise, cholesterol builds up in the arteries, clogging them up so they become narrower. This causes your blood pressure to rise and may lead to heart attacks in later life. Regular aerobic exercise also helps keep your blood sugar level normal. It protects you from developing diabetes, a disease in which the pancreas doesn't produce enough insulin—the hormone that controls blood sugar.

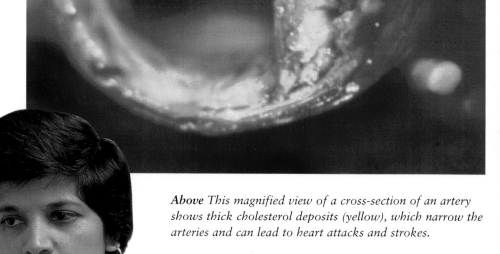

Above This magnified view of a cross-section of an artery shows thick cholesterol deposits (yellow), which narrow the arteries and can lead to heart attacks and strokes.

Left A doctor measures a young girl's height. Regular exercise helps the body develop to its full potential.

7. GROWTH

Because your body is designed for movement and not for sitting around, it grows in the healthiest possible way when it gets plenty of exercise.

8. BODY FAT

When you get aerobic exercise, you burn mostly fat for fuel. Unless you take regular aerobic exercise, you may have quite high levels of body fat—even though you may not look fat. Exercise boosts your metabolic rate for several hours afterward, so you continue to burn more calories than if you hadn't exercised at all. Strength-training also boosts your metabolic rate and helps keep you slim or lose fat if you are overweight.

TRUE OR FALSE?

Exercise makes you eat more.
False. Many people find it hard to eat after exercising, although some people do feel extra hungry. But it is important to refuel as quickly as possible after exercise in order to recover. Best to eat are foods that are rich in natural forms of carbohydrate, such as a banana. Carbohydrate is stored in the muscles and liver for immediate energy. Try to avoid fatty and sugary foods. Fat is stored and used up only when there is no carbohydrate left to burn. Sugary foods give you a temporary burst of energy, but may make you feel more tired later on.

The occasional meal of burger, french fries, and a soda is fine, but it's best not to have too many fried, fatty foods and sugary drinks. Carbohydrates, such as plain potatoes, rice, or pasta, will provide you with all the energy you need for exercise and help you to refuel afterward.

9. POSTURE

Exercise improves your agility, flexibility, and overall posture, so you become more coordinated, graceful, and upright.

10. LUNGS

Regular aerobic exercise strengthens the muscles you use for breathing, making your breathing more efficient. You breathe more deeply but need fewer breaths to take in the same amount of air, so your rate of breathing slows down. This may be why people who take regular aerobic exercise tend to live longer than people who don't —studies have shown that slow-breathing animals live longer than animals that breathe quickly. Improving your lung capacity is also very important if you've got asthma.

11. BONES

When you walk or run, the bones of your legs and spine support your weight against gravity, which tries to pull you downward. This weight-bearing exercise increases the bones' density, making them stronger and less likely to break. When you stand on your hands, the bones in your arms become stronger. And when you lift weights, your bones are strengthened because muscle pulls on bone.

A cross-country runner catches his breath and recovers after a race. Exercise improves your lung capacity. It will gradually make your lungs more efficient and slow your normal breathing rate down.

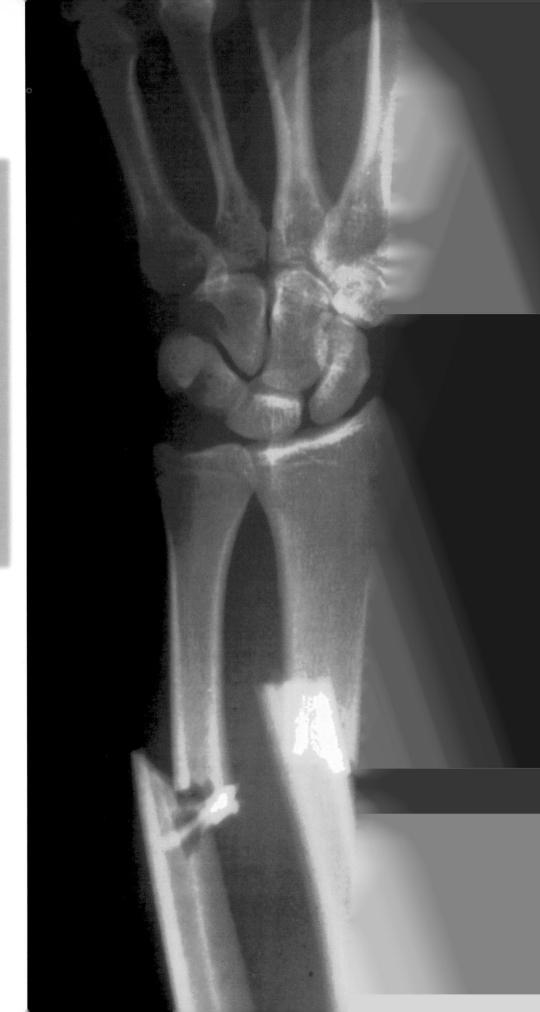

An X-ray image showing broken bones in the lower arm. Higher bone density helps protect against fractures.

BONE DENSITY

Building up bone density is vital when you're young, especially for girls. The stronger a young girl's bones are, the less likely she will be to suffer from osteoporosis (brittle bones) in her fifties and beyond. Around menopause, when estrogen levels fall, bone density is reduced. This can lead to painful fractures, disability, and even death.

12. DIGESTION

Exercise speeds up the passage of food through your body, making you less likely to get constipated. Poisonous residues do not remain in the body, which is probably why exercise protects you against bowel cancer in later life.

13. COMPLEXION

When you exercise, you get hot and sweaty as your body loses heat to keep cool. Sweating improves the blood supply to your skin and keeps the pores clean, which helps your complexion look its best.

14. MUSCLES

Aerobic exercise builds capillaries in your muscles, so that the supply of oxygen-rich blood to the working muscle is improved. When you work on your strength and muscular endurance, you grow more muscle fibers. Having more muscle speeds up your metabolic rate, makes you stronger, gives you more energy, and improves the appearance of your body so it looks more taut and toned.

15. SLEEP

Exercise uses up energy so you sleep better.

16. HEALTH IN LATER LIFE

Because of all these benefits to the body, regular exercise keeps people fit and healthy long into old age. Many problems linked with old age are caused by lack of exercise.

Below Working the abdominal muscles through abdominal curls prevents you from developing a "pot belly" and improves your posture.

For example, most people lose up to 60 percent of their muscle between the ages of 30 and 70. This causes their metabolic rate to slow down and is the main reason why so many people get fat in later life. People who get regular muscle-strengthening exercise do not lose their muscle. They remain strong, agile, and coordinated. They are less likely to suffer from backaches or fall over and injure themselves.

17. LONG LIFE

Regular exercise prevents many of the potentially fatal diseases of later life, including heart disease, stroke, osteoporosis, and some kinds of cancer. Regular exercise delays the ageing process generally, and people who get exercise live longer than people who don't.

If you want a long life, get active! Older people who exercise regularly are more fit, more agile, and less prone to disease than those who never exercise.

TRUE OR FALSE?

Muscle building makes you bigger.

True and false. Once boys reach puberty, training muscles for strength makes them bigger because their bodies have high levels of the hormone testosterone, which promotes muscular growth. Girls, on the other hand, do not bulk up if they do muscle-building activities, because they have low testosterone levels. If they are carrying a lot of body fat, muscle training will actually help them to slim.

PSYCHOLOGICAL BENEFITS OF EXERCISE

As well as improving the physical performance of your body and your general health, exercise can also have a powerful impact on your emotions and mental well-being.

1. MOOD

If you do any form of exercise, you will end up more cheerful than when you started. This is probably because exercise increases the levels of endorphins in your blood. Endorphins are substances produced by the brain to relieve pain and make you feel good.

2. STRESS LEVEL

The changes in your body caused by exercise—and aerobic exercise in particular—leave you less tense, anxious, and stressed than before. Feeling relaxed aids concentration, so it can help you perform better at school. It may help your relationships with other people. The tranquilizing effects of exercise are caused by the fall in blood pressure, heart rate, breathing rate, and skin tension, as well as by the body's being able to get rid of two stress hormones, adrenalin and noradrenalin, more quickly.

3. ENERGY

When you do aerobic exercise, you will notice a leap in vitality that lasts up to an hour after the exercise. You will also feel an energy and alertness that last much longer.

Below Exercise cheers you up—even if you don't win the match! The endorphins produced by exercise, the fun you have while playing the game, and the friendship with your teammates are guaranteed to make you feel good.

4. PROBLEM-SOLVING ABILITY

Exercise not only makes you feel good, but it also distracts you from your worries. It can help you deal with everyday concerns. You may even come up with a solution to a problem when you stop worrying about it and concentrate on working out instead.

5. IMPROVING SELF ESTEEM

If you get regular exercise you'll develop pride in your performance as you get better at what you do. You'll also have more faith in your health—people who exercise have fewer headaches, stomachaches, and sleep problems. And you'll be more likely to believe that you are

Working out puts you in a better mood to deal with problems.

attractive. People who start to exercise regularly find they have greater self esteem than before, because they have more energy, stamina, and grace, and they look slimmer and better toned. This makes them think more highly of themselves.

WHAT IS RUNNER'S HIGH?

Runner's high is a state of euphoria (bliss) that some runners experience after exercising for 20 minutes or more. It is thought to be caused by increased levels of endorphins in the blood.

10. HAVING FUN

Together, all the above factors explain why exercise is fun. If you're used to sitting around, exercise may seem like hard work. If you're not used to it, you will find it tiring at first. But your energy levels will soon rise. Just look at young children and see how much they enjoy physical activity. Find a sport that you enjoy, and you'll remember how much fun it is to move your body.

6. SELF CONFIDENCE

Regular exercise will help you overcome fear. It will help you become more physically confident, and it will encourage you to mix with different people.

7. NEW FRIENDS

Exercise classes and team sports are ideal for getting to know new people. Join a running or swimming club if you prefer solo sports.

8. COMPETING

Healthy competition can help you get better at whatever you enjoy doing. It makes getting fit far more fun. It's also the perfect way of getting rid of your aggression.

9. BRAIN POWER

Exercise pumps up the brain as well as the body. This can be seen in old people who get regular exercise—they remain mentally sharp and are less likely to lose their memory, learning ability, and powers of thought than old people who don't exercise. Any exercise that demands agility, coordination, concentration, rapid reactions, and tactics, such as martial arts and racket sports, is good at stimulating the brain. The mental benefits are caused by the improved flow of freshly oxygenated blood to the brain and the intellectual challenge.

Left Bat-and-ball sports stimulate brain power as well as keeping you fit. Table tennis improves your hand/eye coordination and reflexes.

Below Martial arts such as judo, karate, and tai kwon do can help you grow in confidence, become less timid, and overcome your fears.

GET ACTIVE!

You will become more fit if you simply sit around less and become more active. Walk instead of taking the bus. Speed up your pace instead of dawdling. Meet up with a friend and go ice skating or go for a swim instead of going to see a movie or staying in and playing computer games.

EXERCISE TARGETS

Aim to move your body around for a total of at least an hour every day. Work up to this gradually. You don't have to keep moving for 60 minutes all at once. It doesn't matter if you do 10 minutes here and 15 minutes there. Just try to keep active for one hour altogether.

DON'T OVERDO IT

If you already have a passion for a particular activity, such as roller-blading or football, you won't need much encouragement to do more—in fact, you'll probably want to keep going all day. But over-enthusiasm can be risky. It's easy to overdo things and injure yourself if you always work your body in the same way.

Build up your exercise levels gradually—don't rush it. Even cycling to school or to a friend's house instead of taking the bus or getting a lift in the car is a useful start. Exercise with friends if it makes it more enjoyable, because the more you enjoy it, the more you'll want to keep on exercising.

HOW MUCH EXERCISE SHOULD YOU DO?

★ Aerobic activity (brisk walking, cycling, swimming, most sports, or dance)—aim for one hour a day in total.

★ Muscular training (exercises to strengthen the muscles of the legs, arms, shoulders, chest, back, abdomen and buttocks)—twice a week.

★ Flexibility work (stretching)—twice a week.

CROSS-TRAINING

If possible, you should cross-train to build up your over-all fitness. Remember that improving your over-all fitness involves working at your aerobic fitness, muscular fitness, and flexibility. Cross-training mixes activities with different benefits, such as running (aerobic fitness), weight-training (muscular fitness), and yoga (flexibility). Like this, you can train safely every day. You don't need to follow a rigid training program. Just make sure that you keep on doing a bit of everything.

Right Team sports such as volleyball demand discipline and commitment—and cooperation with your teammates.

ALWAYS WARM UP

If you watch sports on TV, you will have noticed that professional athletes always jog around and stretch their muscles before the main event. They are warming up. Warming up increases the heart and breathing rate gradually, so there is no sudden strain on the heart. It also lubricates joints and raises the temperature of muscles. Warm muscles are more flexible, so they're easier to stretch. Muscles that have been warmed up and stretched are less likely to be injured than tight, cold muscles.

Below Stretching and warming up are essential parts of any form of exercise, because they help prevent injury.

Right Stretching after exercise helps your muscles recover and helps make you more flexible.

WARM-UP TIPS

★ Try to get into the habit of warming up for five minutes and then stretching.

★ Any activity will do to warm up—marching on the spot, gentle jogging, knee bends, and arm-circling.

★ Stretch all the muscles to be used, such as the calf, back of the leg, and front of the thigh.

★ Hold stretches for no more than six to eight seconds.

MAKE SURE YOU COOL DOWN

You will often see professional athletes continuing to jog after finishing a competitive event. They are cooling down. Cooling down is all about slowing down activity gradually. Stopping suddenly strains the heart, which has to work extra hard pumping blood away from muscles. It is easy to stretch when you are still warm. Lengthening muscles helps them recover from the hard work and prevents stiffness the following day. And it is the best time to work on your flexibility.

COOL-DOWN TIPS

★ Try to get into the habit of cooling down for five minutes and then stretching.

★ Do the same exercises as you did to warm up, gradually making your movements more gentle.

★ Put on a sweat shirt and pants to keep warm while stretching.

★ Stretch all the muscles you have been using.

★ Hold stretches for up to 30 seconds.

STRETCHES

Here are some useful stretches to loosen up key muscles before and after exercise.

1 Calf (gastrocnemius and soleus)
Pushing against a wall, extend your right leg behind you (toes forward) and press your heel into the ground. Change legs and repeat.

2 Front of thigh (quadriceps)
Holding on to the wall, take hold of your right ankle or sock and ease it toward your bottom, keeping knees level. Press your hip forward. Change legs and repeat.

3 Back of leg (hamstrings)
Extend the right leg in front and bend forward, keeping your back flat and chest lifted. Place your hands on your bent left leg. Change legs and repeat.

After exercising, do this stretch lying down. Draw the right knee into the chest and gently straighten the leg, holding it at the ankle or calf. Keep head and shoulders relaxed on the ground. Hold the stretch and extend it when the tension eases. If the leg quivers, ease off. Change legs and repeat.

4 Inside leg (adductors)
Sit upright with legs wide apart and feet flexed. Reach for your toes, keeping your back flat.

5 Back of the arm (triceps)
Extend the right arm up and drop it down your back. Take hold of the elbow with the left hand and ease it down. Change arms and repeat.

6 Shoulders (deltoids)
Stretch the right arm in front of you and fold it across your chest, using the left hand to press it in. Change arms and repeat.

7 Upper back (trapezius)
Extend both arms in front and clasp hands, knuckles out. Drop your head, press outward, and try to separate the shoulder blades.

10 Back (erectus spinae and latissimus dorsi)
On all fours, pull your head and bottom together so you round your back. Then raise head and bottom to reverse the stretch. From there, push your bottom toward your heels and extend your arms away from you.

12 Sides (oblique abdominals)
Lying on your back, drop both bent knees to one side, keeping arms outstretched on the opposite side. Change sides and repeat.

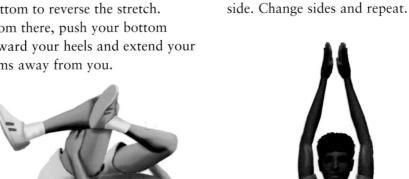

8 Chest (pectorals)
Extend both arms behind and clasp hands, knuckles out. Lift your hands and squeeze the shoulders together.

11 Bottom (gluteus maximus)
Lying on your back, cross the right foot over the left thigh and pull your left thigh in to your chest. Change sides and repeat.

9 Abdomen (rectus abdominus)
Lying on your front, push up on your elbows, sticking your chin out.

13 Full body
Extend your arms above your head and stretch your whole body.

Left *Properly fitting sneakers and socks cushion and support your feet, but keep them for sports, as they will soon wear out and lose their effectiveness if you wear them all the time. Only use them for the activity for which they were designed.*

WHAT TO WEAR

You want to feel comfortable when you exercise, so don't wear anything tight. Take an extra layer to give you warmth afterward. Old T-shirts and a tracksuit or shorts are fine, although you may prefer designer gear.

FABRICS

Cotton clothes absorb sweat and allow heat to escape. Some special sports fabrics draw sweat to the surface of the clothes so it can evaporate. Clothes must also be hard-wearing, because they will get washed many times. Sports socks are made of thicker material than ordinary socks to absorb impacts.

ESSENTIAL ITEMS

★ Girls need a well-fitting sports bra, because vigorous exercise can cause breast pain.
★ Boys need an athletic supporter for all contact sports.

HYGIENE

Always shower after exercise and use your own towel. Sharing towels can spread skin infections. Wear sandals in changing rooms and dry between your toes to prevent athlete's foot. Use a deodorant.

REST AND RECOVERY

Rest is just as important as exercise. The improvements brought about by training for muscular fitness actually take place after exercise, because muscles become stronger while you're resting. Vary aerobic activities from day to day to avoid over-stressing muscles and joints.

TRAINING TIPS

★ Don't train for muscular fitness more than three times a week.
★ Never train for aerobic fitness in the same way, day after day.
★ Avoid intense training, day after day.
★ Slow down or stop (after cooling down) if you're tired.

Below *This image, magnified about 4,000 times, shows thin branches of the athlete's foot fungus growing on human skin. In the center is a skin flake. This infection is easily treated with creams and powders.*

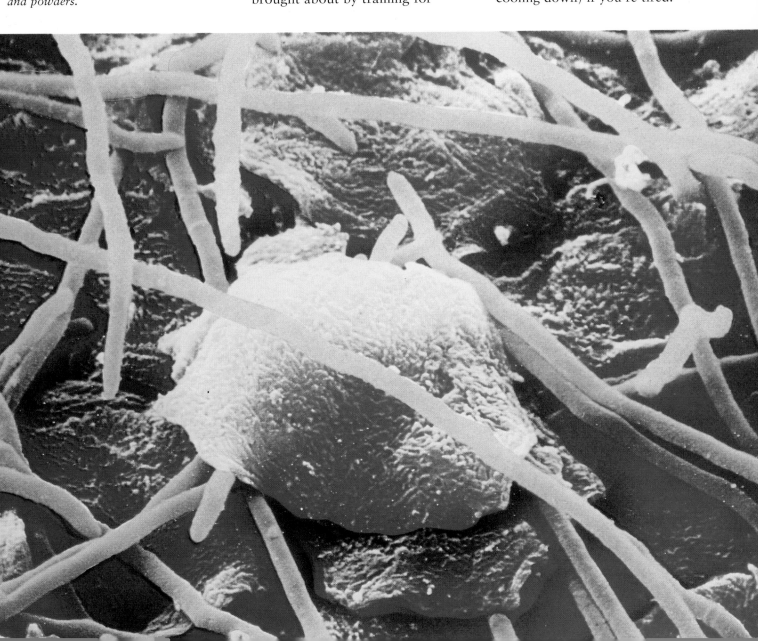

Pasta is a form of carbohydrate popular with many athletes. Some athletes get together and have "pasta parties" to "carbohydrate load" before major events.

FOOD FOR FITNESS

For long-term health, fat loss and energy, follow a Mediterranean-style diet, based on carbohydrates (rice, pasta, potatoes, and bread) and five or more servings of fruits, vegetables, or salad each day. The body needs carbohydrates, which are stored as glycogen, to fuel muscles during anaerobic exercise.

WHAT IS "CARBOHYDRATE LOADING?"

Marathon runners and endurance athletes encourage their muscles to store more glycogen by carbohydrate loading. A week before the event, they train less but increase carbohydrate intake. Up to 40 percent more glycogen can be stored in this way.

DIETARY DOS AND DON'TS

Olive oil is healthier than butter or margarine, but try not to eat much fat. For protein, which helps to build muscles, eat fish, low-fat dairy foods, chicken, nuts, and pulses. Eat less candy and sugary foods, because they often contain fat and artificial additives. Sweets give you instant energy because

they make blood sugar levels shoot up, but the body responds by producing insulin to bring blood sugar down again, so you end up feeling tired.

WHEN TO EAT

Wait at least two hours after a large meal before exercising—particularly swimming—because of the risk of cramps. If you need extra energy, have a carbohydrate snack, such as dried fruit, before physical activity. Try to eat soon after exercising to help muscles refuel.

PLENTY OF FLUIDS

During exercise, you lose fluid through sweat and exhaled air. Dehydration occurs quickly, before you feel thirsty, reducing your performance and putting a strain on your heart, lungs, and kidneys. So drink plenty of water, particularly if it's hot, before, during, and after exercise.

Right It is crucial to drink regularly during long events, such as cycle racing, because dehydration will make your body perform less effectively.

CHOOSING AN ACTIVITY

Everyone seeks something different from exercise. Only you know what it is about a particular activity that you enjoy. But by and large the world is divided into people who enjoy solo sports, such as running, and people who enjoy organized activities, such as team games and racket sports. The more you enjoy something, the more likely you are to keep doing it.

Snowboarding, an activity that is rapidly gaining popularity among young people, is now a Winter Olympic sport.

CLUBS AND CLASSES

If you want to do your own thing but also want to meet people or need help in getting started, join a class or club. There are clubs that offer coaching in all the sports listed in the table. And there is a range of fitness classes (aerobics, step, circuit-training, conditioning, and many other styles), that provide different mixes of aerobic and muscular training plus flexibility work done to music. Choose the right level and introduce yourself to the instructor.

A trainer or coach can give you advice to help you improve your game.

SOLO ACTIVITIES

Choose a solo activity if you're self-motivated, don't like fixed arrangements, and are not seeking competition. Before you start your activity, make sure you understand not only the benefits to your body, but also any risks. Also make sure that you have the right clothing and equipment for that activity.

WHICH SOLO ACTIVITY?

ACTIVITY	MAIN BENEFITS	MAIN RISKS
Walking	Fat-burning, aerobic, leg strength	Accidental injuries
Running	Fat-burning, aerobic, leg strength	Foot, leg, and back problems
Swimming	Fat-burning, aerobic, all-over strength, low stress on joints	Shoulder injuries, infections, non-bone-building
Cycling	Fat-burning, aerobic, leg strength	Knee and back problems, accidental injuries
Rowing/canoeing/kayaking	Fat-burning, aerobic, upper body strength	Back and shoulder problems, drowning
Track and field athletics	Explosive power, leg strength	Leg and groin injuries
Gymnastics	Bone-building, balance, strength, flexibility, explosive power	Joint damage, accidents, overtraining
Trampolining	Strength, coordination, precision	Accidental injury
Riding	Abdominal and leg strength, balance, agility	Accidental injury, lower back problems
Climbing	All-over strength, agility, reflexes, bone-building	Accidents and natural hazards
Snowboarding	Leg strength, coordination, agility	Accidental injury
Skiing	Leg strength, precision, reflexes	Accidents and natural hazards
Skating	Fat-burning, aerobic, leg strength, balance	Leg and groin injuries, accidents
Yoga	Flexibility, strength, serenity	With care, none
Weightlifting	All-over strength, muscle endurance	Muscle injuries

RACKET SPORTS, TEAM GAMES, AND COMBAT SPORTS

If you want the thrill of competing against an opponent, then you want a racket or combat sport or perhaps a team game. Racket sports require precision and hard practice. Combat sports teach you inner discipline and how to look after yourself.

Team games mean working together for the good of the team. They require commitment in terms of time and specific responsibilities, such as attacking or defending.

Above The moves of fencing are based on those taught to swordsmen hundreds of years ago. Contestants score points by striking a target area on their opponent's body with the sword's tip.

Left Although football players are protected by thick "body armor," serious injuries are still common as players hurtle into each other at top speeds.

DID YOU KNOW?

WHICH SPORTS BURN MOST CALORIES?

★ Cross-country skiing and skipping are both extremely intense and burn 560 calories if you can keep going for a full hour—if you weigh 110 lbs. (50 kg).

★ Other intense activities include running, jogging, climbing, squash, skiing, basketball, and soccer.

WHICH GROUP ACTIVITY?

ACTIVITY	MAIN BENEFITS	MAIN RISKS
Racket sports		
Tennis	Hand/eye coordination, leg and racket-arm strength, speed, agility, reflexes, tactics, bone-building	Shoulder, ball injuries
Squash	Hand/eye coordination, leg and racket-arm strength, speed, agility, reflexes, tactics, bone-building	Twisting, lunging, and ball injuries
Team games		
Soccer	Leg strength, speed, explosive power, some aerobic benefits, bone-building, tactics, agility	Contact injuries, leg and groin injuries
Netball/ basketball	Leg strength, speed, explosive power, some aerobic benefits, bone-building, tactics, agility	Contact injuries, knee, ankle, shoulder injuries
Football	All-over strength, speed, explosive power, some aerobic benefits, bone-building, tactics, agility	Very serious contact injuries
Baseball	Leg and arm strength, speed, explosive power, bone-building, hand/eye coordination, timing	Ball/accidental injuries, elbow/shoulder injuries
Hockey	Leg strength, speed, explosive power, some aerobic benefits, bone-building, tactics, agility	Serious leg and stick injuries
Volleyball	Leg strength, speed, explosive power, hand/eye coordination, elevation, reflexes, agility, bone-building, tactics	Ball and accidental injuries, Achilles tendon injuries
Combat sports		
Boxing	Superb overall fitness, aerobic and upper body body strength, hand/eye coordination, bone-building, power, speed, agility, tactics	Potentially fatal injuries
Karate/judo/ tae kwon-do	Flexibility, strength, speed, power, agility, bone-building, self-defense, coordination, tactics, mental discipline	Serious accidental injuries

AVOIDING PROBLEMS

The most likely problem that will occur when you become more active is injuring yourself. Injuries can't be avoided altogether, especially if you enjoy contact sports. But there is a lot you can do to minimize the risk.

CLOTHING AND EQUIPMENT

Many injuries are caused by worn or badly fitting shoes and untied shoelaces. Make sure shoes fit properly. Equipment of the correct size, from bikes to tennis rackets, is essential to avoid putting unnecessary stress on your joints. Use properly fitting protective gear, such as helmets, elbow and knee protectors, gum shields, and athletic supporters.

Above Sports shoes that fit well are essential for avoiding injuries when playing sports.

Left This roller-hockey goalkeeper wears protective padding and a helmet to prevent injury from fast-moving opponents, sticks, and balls.

TRAINING INJURIES

Injuries often occur when you're tired or if you haven't warmed up. You will get tired if you're not fit enough for what you're doing (such as doing an advanced class when you're really a beginner), when you ask too much of yourself (such as running a marathon) when you haven't been eating properly, and when you overtrain.

OVERTRAINING

Excessive training stresses bones, joints, and muscles, and causes injuries that can damage your growth, plague you for years, and keep you from exercising. Overtraining also weakens your immune system, so you start getting lots of colds and other infections. Protect yourself by training for all-around fitness, vary your activities, and run on soft surfaces. Allow for gradual progress and get plenty of rest.

WHAT IS EXERCISE ADDICTION?

Exercise addicts exercise every day; they only feel good when exercising. They feel deprived and miserable if they can't exercise, and they withdraw from friends in order to exercise. One theory is that they become addicted to the high levels of endorphins (the body's own morphine-like substances that make you feel good) produced during exercise. Exercise addiction is sometimes linked with the slimming disease called anorexia, where people become very thin.

HOW MUCH BODY FAT SHOULD YOU HAVE?

★ Young men average 5–20 percent body fat, but young women average 11–30 percent (they need their body fat for fertility).

★ The ideal is around 15 percent for young men and 22 percent for young women.

★ Body fat can be measured by being wired up to a machine called a bio-impedance monitor or having skin folds measured with a giant pair of tweezers called calipers. If you are worried about your body fat, consult your doctor.

ADOLESCENCE

Boys and girls mature at different times. Girls have their growth spurt between 10 and 12, when body fat is stored ready for menstruation to begin. Girls who train strenuously at this time will delay their periods, which does not affect fertility later on, but does affect the strength of their bones.

Right *Many girls worry about their figures. In some cases, they develop distorted self-images, perhaps believing that they are overweight when their weight is in fact perfectly normal. This can lead to eating disorders such as anorexia. If you are concerned about your weight, consult your doctor.*

Adolescent girls often feel self-conscious about their shapes and stop exercising, which causes weight problems. They then try to diet. Most diets fail and can lead to years of disordered eating. Exercise is the best way to burn unwanted fat.

Boys have their growth spurt between 12 and 14, after which they gain strength and lose body fat. Boys should not start lifting heavy weights until their bones have hardened—certainly not before the age of 18.

Above *Children with overweight parents are often overweight themselves because they learn unhealthy eating habits.*

Below *As you become more fit, your body learns to sweat more. In general, boys tend to sweat more than girls.*

DEHYDRATION

Always take a bottle with you so you can drink while exercising. Check your hydration before you start by looking at your urine. If it's dark, it's concentrated and you're already dehydrated, so take a drink. And drink extra amounts after working out.

HOW MUCH SWEAT WILL I LOSE?

Athletes doing intense exercise in the heat can lose 3 to 5 pints (2 to 3 l) of sweat an hour. Most exercisers can expect to lose around 2 pints (1 l) per hour. But everyone is different, and children and old people have lower sweat rates.

GLOSSARY

Aerobic In the presence of oxygen. Aerobic exercise, such as brisk walking, running, and swimming, is good for the heart and lungs. Your aerobic fitness is how long you can keep going at this kind of exercise.

Anaerobic Without oxygen. Anaerobic exercise, such as using resistance machines or doing floor exercises, is good for your muscles. Your anaerobic fitness is how strong your muscles are and how long they can do repetitive work, such as rowing or weightlifting.

Capillary The tiniest blood vessel linking arteries and veins. Capillaries are found everywhere in the body. They replenish cells with oxygen and remove the waste product carbon dioxide.

Carbohydrate Sugars, starch, and fiber, mostly obtained from plants. Carbohydrates supply your body with energy. Dietitians recommend that as much as 60 percent of your diet should consist of unrefined carbohydrates, such as rice, bread, cereals, potatoes, pasta, fruits, and vegetables.

Cells Tiny, living units that make up the human body. There are many different types of cells—such as nerve cells, blood cells, and muscle cells—each designed to carry out a specific task.

Cholesterol A waxy substance formed by the liver and present in foods such as egg yolks and animal fats. When cholesterol builds up in the arteries it can block them, leading to heart disease.

Cross-training Exercising in different ways for different benefits, for example, running for aerobic fitness, weight-training for muscular fitness, and yoga for flexibility.

Dehydration Lack of water. The body needs a constant supply of water, which is lost in exhaled air, urine, and sweat.

Endorphins The body's natural substances that kill pain and create positive feelings. Exercise causes blood levels of endorphins to rise.

Fat-burning Aerobic exercise. Activities such as swimming or running should help you lose weight, because they make you breathless and mostly burn fat for fuel.

Glycogen Carbohydrate stored in muscles and liver ready for converting into energy when you exercise. The body can only store a limited quantity of glycogen, so it is important to keep eating lots of carbohydrates to keep energy levels high.

Immune system The body's network of glands, which protects against disease and ill-health.

Lactic acid A substance produced whenever muscles work anaerobically and burn glycogen. Lactic acid causes local soreness and fatigue. You cannot continue the same exercise until the lactic acid has been dispersed by the blood, which takes just a moment or two.

Metabolic rate The rate at which a resting body uses energy to maintain all its normal functions.

Motor skills Your speed, power, agility, coordination, reaction times, and ability to balance. Motor skills naturally improve if they are part of the exercise you take. You can also work on them individually with specific exercises.

Osteoporosis Brittle bone disease, in which the density of the bone decreases, often resulting in painful fractures and disability. It mostly occurs in women around menopause (the end of female fertility), but it can also develop in men. Anorexics who stop having periods and endurance athletes are prone to osteoporosis.

Overtraining Doing too much of the same kind of exercise, day after day. Overtraining reduces the effectiveness of your performance and leaves you feeling constantly tired. If you overtrain, you will pick up more sports injuries and will be more likely to catch colds and other infections.

Stamina The ability to keep going at any aerobic activity.

Suppleness Flexibility.

Tissue Cells of the same kind are grouped together to form material called tissue. Bones, cartilage, and muscles are all made of different types of tissue.

FURTHER INFORMATION

FURTHER READING

Ballantine, Richard amd Richard Grant. *Ultimate Bicycle Book.* New York: Dorling Kindersley, 1998.

Bennett Paul. *Keeping Fit.* New York: Silver Burdett Press, 1997.

MacLaren, James. *Learn to Surf.* New York: Lyons and Burford, 1997.

McManners, Hugh. *Complete Wilderness Training Book.* New York: Dorling Kindersley, 1999.

Parker, Steve. *The Body and How It Works.* New York: Dorling Kindersley, 1998.

Parsons, Alexandra. *Look Good, Feel Good* (Life Education). Danbury, CT: Franklin Watts, 1997.

Smith, Tony. *The Human Body.* New York: Stoddart, 1995.

Dorling Kindersley's "Youngest Guide" series gives a how-to-do-it introduction to a wide range of sports and exercise activities, including ice skating, tennis, swimming, athletics, gymnastics, martial arts, dancing, snowboarding, riding, inline skating, football, basketball, and baseball.

FINDING OUT MORE

The best way of finding out more about local opportunities for sports and exercise is to pay a visit to your local sports center, swimming pool, or ice rink, where you can ask for details of clubs and classes. Tell the person you speak to what it is that you would like to do, how old you are, and whether you have any experience in the activity.

Public libraries and health food shops also provide information about local activities, such as yoga groups and running clubs, on their notice boards. Some private health clubs and gyms run classes, such as martial arts, for young people, and your school gym teacher may be able to advise you.

The following organizations also provide information and help:

YMCA of the United States
101 North Wacker Drive
Chicago, IL 60606
(312) 977-0031
www.ymca.net
The YMCA is an organization with branches all over the country. It provides a place for children to play and a place for teens to meet and socialize. The YMCA organizes many sports and activities. The Web site will help you locate the YMCA nearest you for more information.

American Fitness Professionals and Associates
P.O. Box 214
Ship Bottom, NJ 08008
(609) 978-7583
American Fitness Professionals and Associates offers many classes for fitness professionals, such as health and fitness certifications and continuing education. The group also publishes several newsletters about health, exercise, and related topics.

Fitness Link
www.fitnesslink.com
This Web page provides information for those who want to get in shape. The organization's resources include articles on nutrition, exercise, fitness programs, lifestyle changes, and more.

INDEX